SCHIRMER'S LIBRARY
OF MUSICAL CLASSICS

Vol. 2058

MUZIO CLEMENTI

Sonatinas and Sonatas

For Piano

Edited and fingered by Giuseppe Buonamici (Op. 2, 12, 24, 25, 33, 34, 40)
and Louis Köhler (Op. 4, 36)

ISBN 978-0-634-09922-9

G. SCHIRMER, Inc.

DISTRIBUTED BY

HAL•LEONARD®
CORPORATION

7777 W. BLUEMOUND RD. P.O. BOX 13819 MILWAUKEE, WI 53213

CONTENTS

SONATINAS, OP. 36

SONATAS

Muzio Clementi
(1752–1832)

In Muzio Clementi's hands, the pianoforte eclipsed the harpsichord in popularity and a new school of piano playing was born. Clementi was among the world's first piano virtuosos, one of several Classical-era composers who helped create the piano sonata, and the first composer to write expressly for the properties of the new pianoforte. A highly regarded teacher and conductor, he was also an astute businessman who manufactured pianos and ran an international music publishing business.

Clementi was born in Rome, began his musical studies at a young age, and became organist at his own church at age 13. When he was 14, a wealthy British man name Peter Beckford "bought" him for a term of seven years. This indentured servitude provided the young musician with a musical and academic education. In 1774, no longer obligated to Beckford, Clementi moved to London, where he began performing as a harpsichordist. However, the advancements made to the pianos of his time soon led him away from the older instrument.

In 1780 Clementi began a concert tour of Europe. On Christmas Eve 1781, Emperor Josef II of Austria staged a musical contest for the entertainment of his guests, pitting Clementi against another famous pianist of the era. The two players were required to improvise and to play some of their own compositions as well as those of other composers. The other competitor was none other than Mozart. The two were quite evenly matched as performers. Mozart was not at all happy about finding a pianistic equal. He made harsh, petty comments about Clementi in letters to his sister Nannerl, calling his colleague a "charlatan" and a "mere mechanicus" (machine). Clementi, however, had nothing but praise for Mozart, saying he had "never heard anyone play with such spirit and grace."

Clementi traveled throughout Europe during his career. Although some of his travels were built around concert tours, others were intended to promote his business interests. He was away from England from 1802 to 1810, creating a market for his pianos and securing the publishing rights to music by various composers. After 1810, Clementi remained in England writing music and building pianos. He was vigorous and remarkably healthy until the very last weeks of his life. He died on 10 March 1832, at age 80, and was buried in the cloisters of Westminster Abbey, a sign of the high regard of his accomplishments in England.

Clementi wrote over 100 piano sonatas during his lifetime which had an enormous impact on composers that followed. His works helped define the sonata-allegro form, a single movement within a sonata (as well as within a symphony, string quartet, etc.) consisting of three sections: the exposition, or statement of the movement's principal themes; the development, in which the composer expands upon, alters, and combines the themes laid out in the exposition; and the recapitulation, in which the exposition is repeated with some changes. The recapitulation is often followed by a coda, which brings the piece to a tidy, decisive conclusion.

Clementi's piano writing foreshadows that of Beethoven, providing a bridge between the Classical and Romantic eras. Beethoven, for his part, had tremendous admiration for Clementi and borrowed the theme from the "Presto" movement of Clementi's Op. 13, No. 6 sonata for the final movement of his *Symphony No. 3, ("Eroica")*. Mozart, while not outwardly complimentary of Clementi, borrowed the opening theme from his Op. 24, No. 2 sonata for the overture to *Die Zauberflöte*. This embittered Clementi to the end of his life, and he placed a disclaimer on any printed edition of this sonata informing the performer that his work was composed 10 years prior to Mozart's opera (see p. 94).

Clementi was the most esteemed piano teacher in London, and his educational works written for students, the *Six Progressive Sonatinas, Op. 36, Introduction to the Art of Playing on the Piano Forte*, and *Gradus ad Parnassum* remain valued teaching tools today. He was in such demand that he once declined an application for lessons from the royal family. Famous for his high fees (reportedly one guinea per lesson), Clementi trained many wealthy pupils, but also taught significant musicians of his day such as J.B. Cramer and John Field. Clementi was also active as a publisher (he was Beethoven's publisher in London). He published the Op. 36 *Sonatinas* in 1797, revising them some 20 years later.

Numbering systems for Clementi works have changed. Further, some pieces at one time identified as Sonatinas are actually now classified as Sonatas.

In this collection:	revised opus number	previous opus number
Sonata in C major	Op. 2, No. 2	Op. 2, No. 1
*Sonata in D major	Op. 4, No. 1	Op. 37, No. 2
*Sonata in E-flat major	Op. 4, No. 2	Op. 37, No. 1
*Sonata in C major	Op. 4, No. 3	Op. 37, No. 3
*Sonata in G major	Op. 4, No. 4	Op. 38, No. 1
*Sonata in B-flat major	Op. 4, No. 5	Op. 38, No. 2
*Sonata in F major	Op. 4, No. 6	Op. 38, No. 3
Sonata in B-flat major	Op. 24, No. 2	Op. 47, No. 2
Sonata in F-sharp minor	Op. 25, No. 5	Op. 26, No. 2
Sonata in D major	Op. 25, No. 6	Op. 26, No. 3
Sonata in A major	Op. 33, No. 1	Op. 36, No. 1
Sonata in F major	Op. 33, No. 2	Op. 36, No. 2
Sonata in C major	Op. 33, No. 3	Op. 36, No. 3

*These were published as Sonatinas in *Schirmer's Library of Musical Classics, Clementi: Sonatinas* (Vol. 40, 50252300). In the present collection these are more correctly labeled Sonatas.

SONATINA.

Muzio Clementi
Op. 36, No. 1

Spiritoso

SONATINA NO. 2

in G major

Muzio Clementi
Op. 36, No. 2

Allegretto

Allegro

SONATINA NO. 3

in C major

Muzio Clementi
Op. 36, No. 3

Spiritoso

Un poco adagio

Allegro

SONATINA NO. 4

in F major

Muzio Clementi
Op. 36, No. 4

Andante con espressione

Rondo
Allegro vivace

Da Capo al Fine.

SONATINA NO. 5

in G major

Muzio Clementi
Op. 36, No. 5

Air Suisse (Original)

Allegro moderato

26

Rondo
Allegro di molto

SONATINA NO. 6

in D major

Muzio Clementi
Op. 36, No. 6

Allegro con spirito

Rondo
Allegretto spiritoso

SONATA
in C major

Muzio Clementi
Op. 2, No. 2

Rondo
Spiritoso

Maggiore

SONATA
in D major

Muzio Clementi
Op. 4, No. 1

Allegro assai

Trio

Men. da capo, senza replica

SONATA
in E-flat major

Muzio Clementi
Op. 4, No. 2

Andantino

Presto

SONATA
in C major

Muzio Clementi
Op. 4, No. 3

Allegro e spiritoso

Allegro

Minore

Maggiore

SONATA
in G major

Muzio Clementi
Op. 4, No. 4

Allegro

Tempo di Menuetto

Andantino

SONATA
in B-flat major

Muzio Clementi
Op. 4, No. 5

Allegro moderato

Rondo
Allegretto

SONATA
in F major

Muzio Clementi
Op. 4, No. 6

SONATA
in B-flat major

Muzio Clementi
Op. 12, No. 1

Larghetto con espressione

VAR. IX

SONATA
in B-flat major

Muzio Clementi
Op. 24, No. 2

Allegro con brio

This Sonata was played by the author before H. I. M. Joseph II., in 1781, Mozart being present.

sempre stacc. il basso

Andante, quasi Allegretto

Rondo
Allegro assai

SONATA
in F-sharp minor

Muzio Clementi
Op. 25, No. 5

Allegro con espressione

Lento e patetico

SONATA
in D major

Muzio Clementi
Op. 25, No. 6

Rondo

Allegro assai

Maggiore

SONATA

in A major

Muzio Clementi
Op. 33, No. 1

SONATA
in F major

Muzio Clementi
Op. 33, No. 2

Presto

8va bassa

SONATA
in C major

Muzio Clementi
Op. 33, No. 3

Allegro con spirito

Adagio e cantabile, con espressione

SONATA
in C major

Muzio Clementi
Op. 34, No. 1

Un poco Andante, quasi Allegretto

This page has been left intentionally blank.

SONATA
in G major

Muzio Clementi
Op. 40, No. 1

Allegro molto vivace

Adagio
Molto sostenuto e cantabile

Canone I, perpetuo per moto retto
Allegro

Canone II, perpetuo per moto contrario

Finale
Presto

SONATA
in B minor

Muzio Clementi
Op. 40, No. 2

Molto Adagio e sostenuto

Allegro con fuoco, e con espressione

Largo, mesto e patetico

SONATA
in D major

Muzio Clementi
Op. 40, No. 3

Adagio molto

Adagio con molta espressione

Minore

Maggiore